Courageous
Women
of the
Bible

Linda Gehman Peachey

MennoMedia

Harrisonburg, Virginia
Waterloo, Ontario

Courageous Women of the Bible
Copyright © 2013 by MennoMedia, Harrisonburg, Virginia 22802.
Released simultaneously in Canada by MennoMedia, Waterloo, Ontario N2L 6H7.
All rights reserved.
International Standard Book Number: 978-0-8361-9726-6
Printed in the United States of America
Cover and interior design by Merrill R. Miller, Copyedit by Lauren Stoltzfus
Cover: detail of drawing by Leonard da Vinci of St. Mary and St. Elizabeth

Unless otherwise noted, Scripture text is quoted, with permission, from the New
Revised Standard Version, © 1989, Division of Christian Education of the National
Council of Churches of Christ in the United States of America.

Hymns referenced in this book are from *Hymnal: A Worship Book* (Faith & Life
Resources, 1992), *Sing the Journey* (Faith & Life Resources, 2005), and *Sing the Story*
(Faith & Life Resources, 2007).

The content for this book was sponsored jointly by Mennonite Women USA and
Mennonite Women Canada.

To order or request information, please call 1-800-245-7894 in the U.S.
or 1-800-631-6535 in Canada. Or visit www.MennoMedia.org.

18 17 16 15 14 13   10 9 8 7 6 5 4 3 2 1

Contents

Preface 5

A Word on the Use of This Guide 7

1. Seen by God: Hagar (Genesis 16 and 21:1-21) 11

2. Disobeying Pharaoh: Shiphrah and Puah
   (Exodus 1:8-22) 15

3. Seeking Justice: Mahlah, Noah, Hoglah, Milcah, and Tirzah
   (Numbers 27:1-11) 20

4. Sustaining Hope: Naomi, Orpah, and Ruth
   (Ruth 1:1-18; 4:13-15) 25

5. Speaking Truth: Huldah (2 Kings 22:8-20) 30

6. Honoring Herself: Vashti (Esther 1:1-12, 16-22). 35

7. Undaunted Faith: Mary, Jesus' Mother (Luke 1:26-56) . . . 40

8. Seeking Wholeness: Woman with a Flow of Blood
   (Mark 5:25-34). 45

9. Speaking Boldly: The Syrophoenician Woman
   (Mark 7:24-30) 50

10. Surprising Witness: The Samaritan Woman
    (John 4:1-42) 55

11. Brave Friends: Mary and Martha
    (John 11:1-44; 12:1-11; Luke 10:38-42) 60

12. Strong Partner: Priscilla
    (Acts 18:1-6, 18-19, 24-28; Romans 16:3-5). 65

13. Honoring Courageous Women (Closing Worship) 70

    About Mennonite Women Canada. 75

    About Mennonite Women USA 77

    About the Writer 79

Preface

*In Christ Jesus you are all children of God through faith . . .
There is no longer Jew or Greek, there is no longer slave or
free, there is no longer male and female; for all of you are
one in Christ Jesus. And if you belong to Christ, then you are
Abraham's offspring, heirs according to the promise.*
—Galatians 3:26-29

As a child, I loved the Bible and church was very important
to me. I believed in Jesus and identified myself with God's
people. Yet, as I grew older I started to wonder where I fit in
the story. So many of the faith heroes I encountered were
men. As a woman, was I truly a child of God and able to claim
these wonderful promises?

Fortunately, over the years I have found many rich stories
about women in the Bible. This discovery has been both distressing and wonderful. Distressing because I had to wonder
why I hadn't heard these stories before. Why had it taken
so long for me to learn about Hagar, Shiphrah and Puah,
Huldah, and Vashti? Why had I heard so little about the
Syrophoenician woman, Martha's friendship with Jesus, and
Priscilla's role in the church?

Nonetheless, it was marvelous to uncover these stories.
It was so reassuring to meet these strong, courageous, and
persistent women who were active throughout the biblical
story. Although often overlooked, they heard God's voice
and moved toward life and healing. In the midst of hardship
and injustice, they kept working together, seeking justice,

speaking truth, and witnessing to God's love for all. Truly, they are models who can provide much encouragement and challenge to us today.

Some of these stories may be difficult to hear, as they probe the harsh realities of loss, violence, and oppression. If any of these sessions touch you in an especially powerful way or bring up painful memories, please find a safe person to walk with you. Also, remember that God is always present. Even when things appear hopeless, God knows and loves you, and longs to bring forth life and healing.

Together, may we join these women on the journey toward God's new creation. May their company give us courage and hope.

Linda Gehman Peachey
Lancaster, Pennsylvania

A Word on the Use of This Guide

Spiritual growth involves learning to know God through the Scriptures and through life experience. Thus, the sessions in this guide begin with a scriptural overview and move to personal experience through the visuals and thoughts of the gathering time. The "Deepening" part of each session returns to reflection on Scripture and is followed by integrating questions that relate the session to our own lives. The closing brings together both scriptural insights and life lessons in an atmosphere of prayer.

Women can use this guide in a variety of ways.

1 . Individual reflection and/or group sharing. Women read the lessons during the week, or at the beginning of the session, and choose one or two questions to ponder. In a group setting, each participant might then share her thoughts and insights with the others. This approach recognizes that group sharing is deeply enriched through time for personal reflection. The role of the leader is to facilitate sharing rather than to "teach" the lessons. The leader will need to focus on one or two questions rather than trying to include them all.

Group participants could be encouraged to journal or use another art form to express their response to the material in each lesson. If the participants enjoy preparing in advance, sharing their previous days' or weeks' reflections would be helpful in challenging one another to new insights about the material.

2 . A more traditional approach. Understanding the makeup of your group is essential to the format you choose as leader. A teaching group is more likely to emphasize the "Deepening" section than the integrating questions, which are quite personal in nature. Here are a few questions that you as a leader might use in order to promote interaction with the material presented in the "Deepening" section:

- How have you understood this passage in the past?

- What is new or different about the ideas presented here?

- What do you find interesting or intriguing?

- What makes you uncomfortable?

- What feelings do you notice as you reflect on this session?

- How might the Spirit be inviting you to grow?

3 . Shorter meditations. The group or individual might want to use only the overview, visuals, and gathering for shorter meditations. Some women might prefer sharing stories and memories sparked by the section on gathering. Others will enjoy responding to the question, "If you were the teacher, what would you emphasize in this lesson, or from this Scripture passage?" Still others might like to read the Scripture, spend a few moments in silent reflection, and close with one of the hymns suggested and the prayer.

Whatever the makeup of your group, pray for spiritual growth in an atmosphere of trust, confidentiality, and respect. As women of faith, may we grow in confidence and wisdom as we receive our gifts from God and share them with others.

Additional note especially for group leaders:

Some of these stories touch on difficult experiences in our lives and may touch people in powerful ways. These lessons may bring to light memories of abuse or violation. Be sensitive and alert to this in your group. Make sure there is a spirit of safety and confidentiality as people may start to share experiences they have never shared before.

Be sure to follow up with those who may appear troubled or find themselves dealing with strong emotions. Make sure these women find someone to talk with who can assure them of God's love and walk with them as they find the resources they need. In some cases, they may need professional help, such as a counselor with training and experience in dealing with child abuse, sexual violence, and/or intimate partner abuse. Resources on these issues, including prayers, stories, and reflections, can also be found on the Mennonite Central Committee Abuse Response and Prevention website, http:// abuse.mcc.org.

one . . . .

Seen by God: Hagar

READING: Genesis 16 and 21:1-21

OVERVIEW

The Bible records two amazing encounters Hagar had with God. In both cases, God intervened to help her survive. In Genesis 16, an angel found her wandering in the desert after she ran away from Sarah. The angel gave her a promise very similar to the one God gave to Abraham: God would multiply *her* offspring into a great multitude. In Genesis 21, God helped her find a well of water and again promised to make her son into a great nation.

Hagar's story is one of both comfort and challenge. On one hand, it reminds us that God sees and cares for everyone, even those who are often ignored or mistreated by society. People like Hagar are not invisible. God sees and hears them and they experience and hear God's voice.

This story invites us to look up and respond when God sees and calls to us. And it challenges us to remember that if we seek to learn God's ways, we must learn to see and hear as God does.

VISUAL: a magnifying glass or pair of eyeglasses

GATHERING

All of us have had times when we've felt invisible, or perhaps misused by others. We also know that many people in our communities exist in the shadows, outside the mainstream and with little influence or power.

Try to recall an experience of feeling alone or in a wilderness of grief or despair. What was that like? How did you experience God? How do you imagine God saw you? Bring those feelings and thoughts to God in prayer. As you reflect on Hagar's story, imagine that God is also seeing and speaking to you, where you are.

DEEPENING

What is especially remarkable about Hagar's story is that she was a female slave. She had no rights of her own and was used by others to serve their interests and needs. Perhaps she had been born into a slave family, or perhaps her parents had to sell her in order to pay a debt. We know she was from Egypt and may have been one of the gifts Pharaoh gave to Abraham after taking Sarah into his harem. Sarah and Abraham then used her to solve their inheritance problems and finally abused and rejected her when her son appeared to threaten their son's status and access to the family's wealth.

Nevertheless, God did not abandon Hagar but saw her situation and gave her the assurance and resources she needed to survive. These images of seeing and hearing are important and point toward how God would later *hear* the groaning of the children of Israel and *see* their "affliction, toil, and oppression."[1] Jesus also promised that even sparrows are not ". . . forgotten in God's *sight*."[2]

God also called Hagar by name. Sadly, Abram and Sarai referred to her only as "slave girl" or "slave woman." But

God's angel used her name, showing her respect and honoring her as a full person.

Fortunately, Hagar was able to see God in this encounter. And she gave God the name "God who sees."[3] This too is quite extraordinary. Usually, God names human beings, such as when God changed Abram and Sarai's names to Abraham and Sarah.[4] But here, Hagar gave God a name, recognizing that God saw her as she was and sought to help her.

It is important to remember these stories, for Hagar is not just a biblical figure from long ago. In many ways, she represents us when we feel alone and in despair. But she also embodies those today who are abused or exploited by others, and find it difficult to escape their situation.

Sometimes people are literally trapped in prison-like conditions. Other times they may find it difficult to survive on their own. No doubt this was Hagar's situation, at least while she was pregnant. It would have been hard for her to survive in the desert and so the first messenger encouraged her to return home, where she would at least have food, shelter, and help through the birthing process.

Too many women and children today are caught in similar situations. For example, immigrant women can be used and violated by abusive husbands or employers because they often depend on these individuals for their immigration status and fear being deported.[5] Or young women may flee their homes to escape abuse from family members. Tragically, some people prey on these runaways by pretending to befriend them, and then locking them up and forcing them into prostitution or selling them to others.[6]

Just as God paid attention to Hagar, God invites us to listen to those around us who are victims of abuse. And just as God did not abandon Hagar, God invites everyone to trust God's love and care for all, including us.

INTEGRATING

1. Recall the experience you identified earlier, when you felt alone or forsaken. Who assisted you during that time or what resources were helpful? How did you experience God and what name would describe that? What else would you like to say to God?

2. Who in your community is most vulnerable to violence or exploitation? To what extent are sexual slavery and human trafficking a problem in your community? How do you see God working in those situations?

3. How does your congregation reach out to those who are struggling with despair, or who live in desperate situations? What additional resources or training would be helpful in this ministry?

CLOSING

Sing or read one of these songs:
> "Nothing Is Lost on the Breath of God" (*Sing the Story* #121)
> "Why Should I Feel Discouraged?" (*Sing the Journey* #103)

Use *Sing the Journey* #143, or pray this prayer:
> *Loving God, thank you for seeing and walking beside us even when we feel alone and forsaken. Help us not to doubt your love but to know always that you want to give us what we need. Like Hagar, help us to hear and see when you call our name. Amen.*

---

[1] Exodus 2:24 and Deuteronomy 26:7.

[2] Luke 12:6.

[3] Genesis 16:13, *New Oxford Annotated Bible* translation note.

[4] Genesis 17:5-6, 15-16.

[5] Kavitha Sreeharsha. "Reforming America's Immigration Laws: A Woman's Laws," June 2010, 6–7, http://www.immigrationpolicy.org/sites/default/files/docs/A_Womans_Struggle_062810.pdf.

[6] Nicholas D. Kristof, "Seduction, Slavery and Sex," *New York Times*, July 15, 2010.

two . . . .

Disobeying Pharaoh:
Shiphrah and Puah

READING: Exodus 1:8-22

OVERVIEW

Shiphrah and Puah lived during a time of great oppression, when the people of Israel were treated as slaves and considered a threat to the Egyptian empire. Although the Israelites had lived in Egypt for several centuries, they were still considered foreigners, outsiders who might join with Egypt's enemies in the event of war. And so, like many supreme rulers, Pharaoh acted to decrease this potential danger and intimidate the people with his ruthlessness.

No doubt, Pharaoh thought he could easily frighten women into obeying his orders. And so he instructed the midwives to kill all the Hebrew baby boys at birth. The Hebrew wording is not clear about whether these women were Hebrews themselves or Egyptians who served as midwives to the Hebrews.

In any case, Shiphrah and Puah chose not to follow Pharaoh's law but to fear God and put God's will first. Certainly, it was not God's will to kill these baby boys or inflict such grief on mothers who had just given birth.

This brief story continues to challenge us today. We too are responsible to discern God's will and honor this even when it conflicts with human laws. We too are encouraged to remember and celebrate those who demonstrate such courage and strength.

VISUAL: a stop sign or other image of resistance

GATHERING

Read this story several times and notice what stands out to you. If you were able to meet Shiphrah and Puah, what would you ask them? What would you ask Pharaoh?

Have you ever been asked to do something you felt was wrong or would violate God's will and your own deepest values? What feelings did you have in that situation? What was your greatest fear? What did you do?

DEEPENING

In imagining Shiphrah and Puah in this situation, one wonders if they knew immediately what to do. Or did they discuss Pharaoh's command between themselves or with other midwives to determine how to respond? No doubt they had every reason to fear Pharaoh. If he was willing to kill babies, he would likely not hesitate to punish them too, perhaps with death. Perhaps he would even want to make an example of them.

Yet, as midwives and as women, Shiphrah and Puah could also empathize with other women. They understood well the costs and joys of carrying children and bringing them to life. They knew this deep in their hearts and could not bring themselves to do as Pharaoh ordered, no matter what the consequences.

Still, their decision to disobey was courageous, particularly if they were not Hebrew themselves. In that case, they would not only be defying their own ruler, they would also be crossing ethnic lines to help those whom their community viewed as threatening and dangerous. One wonders if they rehearsed what they would say or do if Pharaoh found out or questioned them.

Perhaps this is why we know the names of these women. So many women in the Bible, and indeed throughout history, are unnamed. They are invisible to us, or known only through the names of their father or husband. But the names of Shiphrah and Puah were recorded, and we can remember them more easily. Some scholars suggest that since God gave them families, perhaps they became matriarchs of prominent families in Israel. If so, it is still surprising that we know *their* names and not the names of their husbands.

Clearly, the Hebrew people wanted to remember and celebrate these women.

Clearly, the Hebrew people wanted to remember and celebrate these women. They provide us with an example of the value of using our skills and gifts for the good of all. They also remind us that even mighty Pharaoh does not always win, especially when people are willing to revere and obey God instead.

Sadly, there is a harsh note at the end of the story. Shiphrah and Puah were not able to stop Pharaoh's plan completely or end the suffering of these people. In verse 22, Pharaoh commands everyone to destroy the male Hebrew children. The struggle was not over but had to continue in other ways. Now even more people had to decide whether to obey Pharaoh or whether to honor God by helping keep these young boys safe and hidden in their homes.

INTEGRATING

1. Name others from the Bible who also obeyed God over human rulers. Why is it important to remember and celebrate those who have disobeyed human laws in order to honor God?

2. In Anabaptist history, many women and men were quite courageous in living according to their interpretation of Jesus' teachings. Sometimes they challenged laws they felt were unfaithful to God's will. From your understanding of history, name some ways that the early Anabaptists challenged authorities. Today, Mennonites have come to be known as the "quiet in the land" and find it difficult to confront or disobey unjust situations or laws. What are some of the tensions involved in these situations?

3. In your community, are women or men most likely to speak up or resist an unjust situation? Why? What factors lead to action or cause people to hesitate?

4. How does your congregation nurture courage and assist people in following God's will even when this is costly? How might God call people to challenge laws that oppress others?

5. How do you respond to the end of this story? What lessons might we learn from this difficult but realistic endnote?

CLOSING

Sing or read one of these songs:
   "Guide My Feet" (*Hymnal: A Worship Book* #546)
   "Lift Every Voice and Sing" (*Hymnal: A Worship Book* #579)

Use *Hymnal: A Worship Book* #736 or pray this prayer:
   God of life, give us wisdom and courage to do your will.
   Like Shiphrah and Puah, help us care for those who might
   be hurt by unjust laws. Help us follow your way even when
   we have to take risks and do not know where this will lead.
   Amen.

Seeking Justice:
Mahlah, Noah, Hoglah, Milcah, and Tirzah

READING: Numbers 27:1-11

OVERVIEW

The story of Mahlah, Noah, Hoglah, Milcah, and Tirzah is truly remarkable. The leaders of Israel were in the midst of taking a census and dividing the land among the Hebrew tribes. These sisters realized that since their father had died and there were no sons, their family would get nothing, and his name would be lost to the future. So they dared to ask for a change in the inheritance laws so that women could inherit land when a family had no sons.

This request is especially amazing because it came soon after a dramatic showdown between Moses and Korah and his followers. As punishment for this rebellion, the earth opened up and swallowed several hundred people, and a plague ravaged the rest of the community. The people were very afraid, and they said to Moses, "Everyone who approaches the tabernacle of the Lord will die. Are we all to perish?"[1]

Despite all this, these sisters found the courage to come to the tabernacle and stand before Moses and the rest of the congregation, asking that they be given a portion of the land being divided among the Israelite clans. Moses took their request to God, who answered that these women were indeed right and they should be given their father's inheritance.

VISUAL: a sturdy post, representing courage, or a braided rope, symbolizing strength in joining together

GATHERING

Read this passage and try to imagine being one of these sisters. What kind of conversation would you have had with each other? Whom would you be? Would you be one of those urging the need to speak up, or one who thought it was too daring or too foolish to make such a request?

Recall a time when you felt something was terribly unfair or unjust. Try to identify the feelings you had. Were you able to pray about this concern or discuss it with anyone? What was most helpful or unhelpful?

DEEPENING

One of the most significant aspects of this story is that these sisters acted together. Surely they experienced much disagreement and doubt, and one can imagine them having many conversations about whether to do anything or not. When they did decide to act, they had to figure out what to do, when to do it, and who would speak first.

Interestingly, the Bible doesn't say who spoke. These women are presented as a unit, standing together in a common bond of sisterhood. No one opted out; they were all there, giving themselves and their request added strength.

It is also impressive that these sisters spoke up publicly, before everyone. They did not try to go to Moses privately or through an intermediary, but spoke about their concern right out in the open, in front of all the people. One wonders if they feared what people would say or that they might be labeled brazen or too bold. Yet, while they may have felt intimidated and afraid, they did not allow their fears to have the last word but acted together for what they felt was right.

While they may have felt intimidated and afraid, they did not allow their fears to have the last word but acted together for what they felt was right.

Fortunately, God affirmed their request and the community honored it as well. This was so significant, in fact, that these sisters are mentioned four other times in the Hebrew Scriptures: Numbers 26:33; Numbers 36:1-12; Joshua 17:3; and 1 Chronicles 7:15.

Of course, women still did not have equal rights with men. Women who inherited land this way were required to marry within their father's tribe, so the land would not be transferred out of the tribe's ancestral holdings. Nevertheless, within these guidelines, God gave these sisters permission to "marry whom *they* think best."[2]

Tragically, women still struggle with questions of land and inheritance. Studies show that while women represent over 50 percent of the world's population and grow nearly half the food in the developing world, many do not have secure rights to the land they farm.[3]

This has important consequences not only for women, but for their children and communities. When women have access to income and family assets, their households tend to have better nutrition and health. Children are more likely to go to school and women are less vulnerable to contracting HIV/AIDS. Secure land rights also increase women's status and bargaining power within the household and community, and provide them greater incentives to adopt sustainable farming practices and invest in their land.[4]

INTEGRATING

1. Recall the experience you identified earlier, of seeing or experiencing a situation that cried out for justice. What did you do in that situation? What was the result and what did you learn? How do these sisters speak to that situation, or not?

2. Questions of inheritance continue to be an important issue and many today deal with family situations that seem unfair. How has this been handled in your family? What feelings or thoughts have you had? What has been helpful? Who were like these sisters and helped you work through the situation?

3. How does discernment happen in a group? How do we think together about what God is saying and when God wants us to act?

4. Where do you see situations of economic injustice in your community? Who is responding to those needs and how? Is it important that everyone have fair access to economic resources? Why or why not?

CLOSING

Read this litany around the circle, one person reading each line (from *Sing the Story* #200):

In the face of all our realities:
we are the people who heal each other,
who grow strong together,
who name the truth,
who know what it means to live in community,
moving towards a common dream
for a new heaven and a new earth
in the power of the love of God,
the company of Jesus Christ,
and the leading of the Holy Spirit.

Sing or read one of these songs:

"For the Healing of the Nations" (*Hymnal: A Worship Book* #367)

"God of Grace and God of Glory" (*Hymnal: A Worship Book* #366)

....

[1] Numbers 17:13.

[2] Numbers 36:6.

[3] "Landesa Center for Women's Land Rights," Landesa Rural Development Institute, http://www.landesa.org/women-and-land/.

[4] Ibid.

Four . . . .

Sustaining Hope:
Naomi, Orpah,
and Ruth

READING: Ruth 1:1-18; 4:13-15

OVERVIEW

When studying this story, people have tended to focus on Ruth, the daughter-in-law who stayed with Naomi and helped her return to Bethlehem. Yet it is important to remember Orpah too, and the difficult choices faced by all of these women. All three represent the lives of many women today: women who face famine and the loss of family members, women who have no secure means of support and migrate from place to place seeking food and safety, and women forced to choose between their homeland and life in a foreign country.

This is also a story about friendship and solidarity between women. Although Naomi felt God had turned away from her and left her empty, her daughters-in-law had not abandoned her. Both showed deep love and affection for her. And when Naomi chose to return to her home country, Ruth went with her and helped her survive.

These women help us reflect on choices we face and the need to value women's work and friendships. We can also learn more about caring for one another across nations and cultures.

VISUAL: a candleholder with figures joining hands around the candle, or a picture of women united in some way or focused on some task in common

GATHERING

Reflect on what it might have felt like to be Naomi, Orpah, and Ruth. What might you have done in their situation? With whom do you identify most? Would you have chosen to stay in your home community or to move into the unknown?

This story also invites us to remember our own experiences of loss. How have we dealt with these and the feelings of pain and abandonment that often accompany them? What kind of support was needed and who helped provide those resources? How have we found hope and the strength to go on with life?

DEEPENING

It is amazing how often the Scriptures urge caring for widows, orphans, strangers, and those who are poor. Over and over again, the Bible urges giving them justice and access to the resources they need.[1] Nevertheless, widows must have had a tough life. Without a man's support they were vulnerable, always at risk of being neglected or harmed.

Naomi seemed to feel this keenly. After her husband and sons were gone, she felt she had nothing left and thought they should all try returning to Judah. One wonders what took place next. Did something terrible happen? Had they run out of food or water? Were they attacked by bandits?

Whatever the case, Naomi stopped their journey and urged Orpah and Ruth to return home. She was convinced the only hope for them was to find new husbands who could support them. And since she could not provide this, she felt she was of no value to them any longer. She felt God had turned against her and life had become bitter.

This is so tragic. Naomi had experienced so many losses that she found it difficult to see what she had left, or truly appreciate how important Orpah and Ruth were to her and she to them. No doubt, she also knew that her society did not really value women or expect they could work to support one another.

Is this why Orpah decided to return to her mother? Perhaps she understood Naomi's realism or feared her despair. Or perhaps she simply longed for her home and the support provided by that community.

It is not always best to leave one's home behind to search for a new life in a new land. It is not always right to ask people to reject their own traditions and adopt foreign ways.

Laura Donaldson, a Cherokee writer, argues we should honor Orpah's choice.[2] Sometimes women need to choose their own family and community. It is not always best to leave one's home behind to search for a new life in a new land. It is not always right to ask people to reject their own traditions and adopt foreign ways. So Orpah can represent those who need to affirm their own people and identity.

Of course, we also want to honor Ruth, who stayed with Naomi as they traveled back to Bethlehem. Once there, Ruth proved strong and brave, as she gleaned in the fields after the reapers gathered the grain. Although the law encouraged this practice, everyone seemed to expect she could be harassed or chased out of the fields.[3] She was also quite surprised by Boaz's kindness, especially to a foreigner like herself.[4] Clearly, it was not an easy task for Naomi and her to make a new life for themselves in Bethlehem.

In the end, the women of Bethlehem reminded Naomi how much God had blessed her because of the "daughter-in-law who loves you, who is more to you than seven sons"[5] With Ruth's love and devotion, along with the support of the larger community, Naomi was encircled once more with family and hope. She was no longer empty but filled with good things.

INTEGRATING

1. Who in your community are most like Naomi, Orpah, and Ruth, needing assistance or protection from harassment or neglect? How do we show solidarity to one another, whether we are women or men, strangers or family members?

2. Like these women, all of us have experienced losses: a loved one, a job, a home, a church community. What losses have been most difficult? How have we dealt with bitterness or the feeling that God has abandoned us? Who or what was most helpful in finding hope and new life? How can we gain strength from friends and family members?

3. In this story, Orpah and Ruth made different choices. How do we honor one another's decisions, especially when they are not the same?

CLOSING

Sing or read one of these songs:
    "Help Us to Help Each Other" (*Hymnal: A Worship Book* #362)
    "Will You Let Me Be Your Servant" (*Hymnal: A Worship Book* #307)

Close with this prayer[6] from *Hymnal: A Worship Book #750*:

> *Gracious God,*
> *we thank you for gifts that belong not to us alone,*
> *but to all our sisters and brothers,*
> *since they, too, are created in your image.*
> *Let their need become our need;*
> *let their hunger become our hunger;*
> *and grant to us also a portion of their pain,*
> *so that in sharing ourselves,*
> *we discover the Christ who walks*
> *with our brothers and sisters. Amen.*

[1] See, for example, Deuteronomy 24:10-21 and Leviticus 19:9-10, 13-17.

[2] R. S. Sugirtharajah, "Postcolonial Biblical Interpretation," in *Voices from the Margin, Interpreting the Bible in the Third World*, ed. R.S. Sugirtharajah (Maryknoll, NY: Orbis Books, 2006), 76–77.

[3] Ruth 2:2, 8-9, 22.

[4] Ruth 2:10-13.

[5] Ruth 4:14-15.

[6] Kenneth I. Morse, *We Gather Together*, copyright 1979 by the Brethren Press. Used by permission.

Five . . . .

Speaking Truth: Huldah

READING: 2 Kings 22:8-20

OVERVIEW

Huldah is one of several women prophets mentioned in the Bible. Others include Miriam (Exodus 15:20; Micah 6:4), Deborah (Judges 4–5), Noadiah (Nehemiah 6:14), Isaiah's wife (Isaiah 8:3), Anna (Luke 2:36-38), and Philip's four daughters (Acts 21:8-9).

One surprising aspect about Huldah's ministry is that it does not appear at all unusual, but rather taken for granted. No one raised an eyebrow about consulting with a female prophet. Apparently, she was well known in the community, even to the king and his court, as someone who knew and could speak for God.

It is also significant that Huldah was asked to pass judgment on a written text. Was this book authentic? Was it God's word or not? Fortunately, she was able to do this and thereby participated in the long process of discerning what would belong in the canon of the Bible.

Huldah was courageous too, able to share honestly about the judgment that awaited the nation. She did not hesitate or sugarcoat her message, but spoke forthrightly and with authority. Her words then spurred further religious reform and revival as the king responded to her message.

In all these ways, Huldah provides a good role model for women today who are called to seek God's will and share it with others.

VISUAL: a Bible or scroll

GATHERING

Consider the women prophets noted above. What have you heard about them? If you could talk with one of them, whom would you choose and what would you ask her? What would you like to know about her and her ministry? Also, think about women in your community to whom people go for advice. While they might not be called prophets today, how do these women help others discern God's will and share God's word?

Finally, try to imagine yourself in Huldah's shoes as these five prominent men came to the door. What questions might you have? What thoughts or feelings arise as they share about the book of the law found in the temple and as you consider your response?

DEEPENING

Scholars think the scroll mentioned here contained an early version of the book of Deuteronomy, especially Deuteronomy 6:13-15 and 28:15-46. Those passages describe what will happen to those who disobey God's laws and worship other gods. In this case, King Josiah was spared seeing Judah's final destruction. Yet, the Babylonian Empire did take control of Judah some 20 years after his death. They carried away the temple's treasures, destroyed the city, and deported many of the people into a long exile.[1]

Certainly, the people of Judah were living in difficult times, trying to survive in the midst of larger empires that surrounded them. No doubt they found it hard to discern how to obey God, provide for their families, and find safety. Like us, they were no doubt tempted to accommodate those who promised other ways of finding security and well-being, rather than relying on what God offered.

Like us, the people of Judah were no doubt tempted to accommodate those who promised other ways of finding security and well-being, rather than relying on what God offered.

Fortunately, the people of Israel had a prophetic tradition that included voices other than kings and priests. Prophets often challenged political and religious leaders and the status quo those leaders sought to maintain. Prophets like Huldah explained God's will and reminded the leaders they were to serve the people as God intended.

Perhaps this is why Huldah initially referred to the king as "*the man* who sent you to me." She did not give him special treatment and reminded everyone that in God's eyes, he was a man like any other. Even the king was subject to God and should not expect extra rights and privileges.

Huldah also did not back down from a difficult message. She spoke clearly and strongly about God's wrath and coming judgment on the people. It is a stern speech, and one wonders how the king's messengers felt as they received it and had to take it back to the king.

It is still uncomfortable to hear these words. Yet, as one reads about the kings who preceded Josiah, one can understand why God was upset. King Manasseh, who ruled for 55 years, is described as one of the wickedest. He reintroduced pagan worship to Judah and set up idols even in the temple. He also practiced child sacrifice, making "his son pass through fire" and "shed very much innocent blood, until he had filled Jerusalem from one end to another."[2]

Although Josiah undertook much reform, even he ended up perishing in a battle against Egypt. And the kings after him continued to do evil and lead Judah into hopeless rebellion against the larger nations around them. All of this ended badly, and one wonders how to interpret such disaster. Was God punishing Judah, or was their long captivity and exile into Babylon the inevitable consequence of their destructive choices? How do we understand God's will in the midst of misfortune and our fallen world?

INTEGRATING

1. How do we discern God's will in the midst of competing voices? Who helps us in this process? To whom do you go to help better understand God's will and how we should live?

2. Who is speaking a prophetic message today? Name those in your church or nation who play a role similar to Huldah's place in her community.

3. If you were Huldah, what message would you give to our leaders today? What kinds of decisions do you fear will lead to suffering and disaster?

4. How do you explain misfortune? When is it a result of God's actions, a consequence of bad choices, or an effect of living in a fallen world?

CLOSING

Sing or read one of these songs:
"This Little Light of Mine" (*Hymnal: A Worship Book* #401)
"How Can We Be Silent" (*Sing The Journey* #61)

Read together litany #138 in *Sing the Journey*. Alternatively, bring to God in prayer the concerns mentioned in response to the third question, and ask for God's wisdom and mercy.

....
[1] 2 Kings 24–25.
[2] 2 Kings 21:6 and 16.

Six . . . .

Honoring Herself:
Vashti

READING: Esther 1:1-12, 16-22

OVERVIEW

Although mentioned only briefly in the Bible, Vashti was a strong woman who dared to stand up for herself and what she felt was right. Her story also presses us to consider whether women have the right to their own self and integrity or must always comply with their husband's commands even when these are unreasonable or dangerous.

Certainly, there have been many changes in women's lives over the centuries. However, women and girls still struggle for equal access to education and fair pay. They still suffer high rates of abuse, violence, and exploitation. They continue to be treated as sex objects in advertising and pornography. Queen Vashti's example can give us courage to take a stand for women and for our own self-respect.

VISUAL: several photos of strong women and girls in your community

GATHERING

Read this passage at least twice and try to picture the setting. What words and images stand out to you? What feelings do you have? Why do you think Queen Vashti refused the king's order to show herself to the people?

While this story can seem very foreign to our experience, consider how women today are asked to do similar things. In what ways are women valued primarily for their beauty? In what situations are they expected to obey without question, even when this is harmful to their well-being?

Perhaps this story reflects your own experience too well, and you too have had to submit to demands that felt wrong or dangerous. If so, find someone to talk with who can assure you of God's love and walk with you as you seek healing. Prayers, stories, and resources can also be found on the Mennonite Central Committee Abuse Response and Prevention website: http://abuse.mcc.org.

DEEPENING

This is truly a difficult text for women. It is also disturbing for men, as they are portrayed in negative and troubling ways in this story. First, the officials and ministers were feasting and drinking for six months. At the end, the king hosted a larger, seven-day banquet for all the men in the city while the queen hosted the women. For the men at least, the emphasis seemed to be on drinking "without restraint," doing "as each one desired." It doesn't take much imagination to picture a scene growing increasingly raucous and out of control.

Finally, when the king was quite drunk, he ordered Queen Vashti to appear and show off her beauty. Although the text is not clear, some translations suggest she was ordered to appear naked before the crowd.[1] Other scholars suggest that wives would not normally be present at such a drinking party—only concubines or prostitutes would.[2] In either case, the request to appear before these men must have felt degrading and even dangerous. After all, these men had been drinking for months and were not in a good position to be respectful or courteous, even to the queen. Deep in her bones, Vashti must have known she would be reduced to little more than a sexual object.

Deep in her bones, Vashti must have known she would be reduced to little more than a sexual object.

Little wonder, then, that she refused to go, despite the risks. Surely, she knew the consequences could be severe, as the king's orders were binding. This king in particular was known in history for not permitting any disagreement.[3]

Here again, the men acted in unflattering ways. Not only was the king drunk and brazen, but his closest advisors appeared to be insecure and paranoid, fearful that this one act of independence by the queen would cause a full-scale rebellion among the women, "with no end of contempt and wrath."[4]

Why were these men so anxious? Were women becoming more assertive? Were they fed up with having the men come home drunk from this endless party? Or perhaps they were tired of being valued only for their beauty and the sexual favors they were asked to perform. From Esther 2:12, we know that women in the harem underwent a year's worth of cosmetic treatments, and perhaps these women were growing restless, no longer willing to be treated only as bodies groomed for the pleasure of men.

In the end, both Esther and Vashti were women who took risks for themselves and others. Although Esther is portrayed as more compliant, she challenged one of the most powerful men in the kingdom. She also persuaded the king to allow some flexibility in the implementation of his decree so the Jews would not be destroyed.

We do not know if Vashti and Esther ever met, but it is intriguing to imagine what they might have said to each other. Did Esther gain strength from Vashti's courage, and did Vashti take comfort in knowing she had done the right thing, perhaps giving Esther an example to follow?

INTEGRATING

1. Where are women today treated primarily as bodies, for the use and pleasure of men? How can the church address this concern?

2. Many women and children experience abuse or violence from family or community members. What resources are available in your congregation and community to respond to and prevent abuse? What resources can help bring healing to survivors?

3. How can we teach our daughters the importance of self-respect and the courage to value their whole beings: body, mind, and spirit? What stories and resources have been especially helpful? Also, what should we teach our sons about women and themselves?

4. When is it important for women or children to honor themselves even if this means disobeying a spouse or parent? What factors make this difficult or even dangerous? How can the church be helpful?

CLOSING

Sing or read one of these songs:
"New Earth, Heavens New" (*Hymnal: A Worship Book* #299)
"For the Healing of the Nations" (*Hymnal: A Worship Book*
#367)

Close by praying this prayer[5] from *Sing the Journey* #154:
Victorious God,
who breaks the powers that strangle and bind us,
liberate your people
so we may join hands to dismantle what divides and
destroys us.
In the strong name of Jesus. Amen.

---

[1] According to Sidnie Ann White, this is spelled out in the *Targum*, the Aramaic translation of the Hebrew Bible. "Esther," in *The Women's Bible Commentary*, ed. Carol A. Newsom and Sharon H. Ringe (Louisville: Westminster/John Knox Press, 1992), 127.

[2] Andre LaCocque, *The Feminine Unconventional: Four Subversive Figures in Israel's Tradition* (Minneapolis: Fortress Press, 1990), 55.

[3] It was even reported that he tried to beat and imprison the sea for "wronging" him! See Carol Lakey Hess, *Caretakers of Our Common House* (Nashville: Abingdon Press, 1997), 21.

[4] Esther 1:18. Carol Lakey Hess argues that everyone benefits when both women and men share their wisdom and make decisions together. The goal is not to become masters of the house (as in Esther 1:22) but *caretakers* of a shared community. *Caretakers of Our Common House* (Nashville: Abingdon Press, 1997).

[5] Copyright © Lois Siemens, Superb Mennonite Church, Kerrobert, Saskatchewan.

Seven . . . .

Undaunted Faith: Mary, Jesus' Mother

READING: Luke 1:26-56

OVERVIEW

This passage introduces us to Mary, the young woman who became Jesus' mother. While the Gospels mention her only a few times after Jesus' birth, we know from Acts that she was also a disciple who met with the believers in Jerusalem.

What is especially remarkable about Mary is her speech to Elizabeth. Given her life situation, it is amazing how exultant and joyful she is. Despite so much evidence to the contrary, she declared that God shows favor to those who are lowly, who hunger and are sent away empty.

How can this be? Somehow, Mary expresses faith not in what she sees, but in who God is and what God wants for the world. The God she worships does not bless the violence, poverty, and death she sees around her, but is acting to change the world.

VISUAL: a selection of paintings or statues of Mary

GATHERING

What have you have heard about Mary? What words, images, or feelings first come to mind?

Read all the Gospel accounts in which Mary appears.[1] What picture does this give you about her and her role in Jesus' life and among the disciples? If you could talk with Mary, what would you want to say or ask her?

DEEPENING

While many paintings of Mary show her in rich robes, it is important to remember she was likely very poor. She had to give birth in a stable, and when it was time to make sacrifices in the temple, she and Joseph could only afford two doves, rather than a lamb and a dove.

She also lived under foreign occupiers who demanded the people be counted in order to tax them more accurately. Even though she was in her last months of pregnancy, she had to make the long, difficult trip to Bethlehem, a journey of over 80 miles.

In addition, her people feared and experienced much violence. She and Joseph had to flee to Egypt as refugees in order to avoid Herod's soldiers, and they still had to be careful about where they settled when they returned to Palestine.

In many ways, Mary was similar to women in impoverished and oppressed communities today, both here and around the world. She too was from a place scorned by others: Galilee, known as backward and religiously questionable, where people did not observe the law properly.[2]

Thus, Mary may have been viewed much like many in our society think about young mothers on welfare or immigrant women who don't have the proper documents. All too often, these women are described as lazy, immoral, and unwilling to take responsibility for their lives.

Like Hannah before her, Mary had faith that God was turning things upside down.

Fortunately, Mary believed deeply in God's love for her and her people. She refused to accept the harsh view of herself that the dominant powers of her day would likely have given her. Despite the fact that Mary was a young, unwed, and marginalized mother, God was blessing her and her people. Like Hannah before her, she had faith that God was turning things upside down.[3] God was giving her a child who represented hope, joy, and life.

Ruby Sales, an early leader in the civil rights movement, explained it this way:

> Mary is more than a young girl with unrealistic expectations. . . . She is a prophet and witness who sees the fertile land of freedom in the arid desert of Roman imperialism. And, she is willing to work to bring this freedom land into being even when there is very little evidence except God's promise that it will come. In this spirit, she sees her pregnancy not as an occasion to despair but as a grace-filled moment. Mary is in harmony with many women in her community who see children as gifts and assets that the community can depend on to push forward their struggle.[4]

Indeed, Mary's speech is not only a statement of faith but a commitment to participating in God's work for justice over many generations. Being Jesus' mother—and a disciple—meant real consequences in her life.

Almost right away, she saw Jesus get into trouble with religious and political leaders. And at the end, during those terrible days in Jerusalem, she had to watch, heartbroken and horrified, as Jesus was arrested and then crucified.

Yet, she also saw God act in miraculous ways, as Jesus shared bread and brought forgiveness and healing to so many who had felt cast aside. It was a movement of great renewal, promising hope and restored relationships. After the resurrection, this movement continued to grow as the disciples worshiped God with joy, shared generously with one another, and reached out to welcome others in.

Certainly, Mary could not envision at the outset where her encounter with Gabriel would lead. She did not know just how much her own world would be turned upside down. There must have been times when she doubted God's love and whether God had indeed blessed her. Nevertheless, she continued to follow, committed to Jesus and the ways of God no matter what.

INTEGRATING

1. How do you respond to Mary's speech? Where do you see God lifting up the lowly and filling the hungry with good things? How does your congregation participate in this work of turning things upside down, of blessing those in our society who are like Mary?

2. Write your own song of faith in God. What are you grateful for? Where do you see God changing our world?

3. What strengthens your faith and enables you to see God's love at work in your life, even in the midst of challenges?

CLOSING

Pray the prayer in *Sing the Story* #134 or ask women to share words of gratitude to God for Mary's life and testimony.

Sing or read one of these songs:
"My Soul Cries Out" (*Sing the Story* #124)
"My Soul Is Filled with Joy" (*Sing the Journey* #13)

....
[1] Matthew 1–2; Mark 3; Luke 1–2; John 2; 19:25-27; Acts 1.

[2] See John 1:46 and 7:40-52, where many argue that no prophet could come from Galilee.

[3] 1 Samuel 2:1-10.

[4] Ruby Sales, unpublished letter, December 2007.

Eight . . . .

Seeking Wholeness: Woman with a Flow of Blood

READING: Mark 5:25-34

OVERVIEW

One reason Jesus got into so much trouble with the religious rulers was his willingness to disregard purity and Sabbath laws. These were the customs and traditions that determined who was considered proper, holy, and faithful; who was in and who was out.

Understanding these laws helps reveal how Jesus' healing miracles provided more than a physical cure. They also brought people back into the community, making them feel welcome and included. Healing provided assurance that illness was not God's punishment for sin but the result of poverty, exploitation, or simply living in an imperfect world that includes disease and misfortune.

The story of this woman's courageous, persistent faith and Jesus' strong love encourages and challenges us to seek and share God's healing power.

VISUAL: small bowl of anointing oil

GATHERING

Read Leviticus 15:19-30 and then the Mark passage. Try to imagine what this woman's life was like. Where did she live and with whom? Who were her friends? How would healing change her life?

If you are in a group, act out this story while someone reads the Mark passage. What do you notice? What emotions does this story stir in you?

DEEPENING

In order to appreciate the power of this story, it is important to understand how bodily discharges were considered unclean in the culture of the time. While there may have been good reasons for these laws initially, they had come to isolate people from one another in unhelpful ways. For women, purity laws meant they were considered unclean and unable to participate in normal community life for seven days of every month: a significant portion of their adult lives.

In the case of this woman, it is hard to imagine how she survived or found the strength to go about her daily tasks. Likely, she had long ago removed herself from contact with others and become an outcast in the community. Her only hope was to make the bleeding stop so she could undergo the purification rituals that would allow her to reenter public life.

No doubt this is why she tried so hard to find healing, spending all her resources on doctors who claimed they could help her. Remarkably, there is no suggestion here that she was so sinful God had refused to cure her. Rather, Mark implies she was a victim, exploited by many physicians even as her condition grew worse.

Scholars note that the Greek word for "be made well" (used in verses 23, 28, and 34) includes the "idea of rescue from impending destruction or from a superior power."[1] Surely, this disease must have felt like a strong force, binding her up and intent on ruining her completely.

Still, it is surprising that this woman dared to touch Jesus. Women were not to touch men outside their families at any time, especially not a woman in her condition. This would make Jesus unclean too. No wonder she trembled in fear when he asked who touched him! She had broken all these taboos. Even worse, she did it while he was on his way to helping a leader in their synagogue.

But Jesus did not chastise her. Instead, he called her "daughter." She was healed! She was part of the family once again. While she may have preferred to slip away quietly, Jesus made sure the whole community knew she had been healed and was no longer a threat to anyone. Not only that, Jesus commended her faith. Whereas the disciples had just shown "no faith,"[2] this destitute woman demonstrated true faith in Jesus that led to healing.

It is important to note that these touches did not result in contamination but in wholeness. As Ched Myers notes, "Jesus both violates and reverses the contagion by his 'touching.'"[3] This had occurred earlier when Jesus touched and healed a leper.[4] It happened with this woman's touch and Jesus' compassionate response. And it took place again as Jesus touched Jairus's young daughter and restored her to life.[5]

One wonders how Jesus had such courage. Perhaps he understood all too well how terrible it was to be excluded and isolated. No doubt he also believed strongly in the power of love to overcome fear and exclusion.

INTEGRATING

1 . In what ways do you identify with this woman? How is it difficult to understand her life experience?

2 . Our society no longer practices these purity laws, yet some people are still held at a distance, unwelcome in many social settings. Who are these people? Where can they find healing? Who offers them hope and friendship?

3 . What experiences have you had that demonstrate the power of love over fear?

4 . Human touch is powerful and can easily be misused. What elements constitute healing touch? When does touching violate and wrong another?

CLOSING

Sing or read one of these songs:
   "Don't Be Afraid" (*Sing the Journey* #105)
   "Christ's Is the World" (*Sing the Journey* #62)

If your group is comfortable and all agree, pass the bowl of oil around the circle. As each woman holds it, she may turn to the woman next to her and anoint her forehead, saying: "You are known and loved by God. You are God's beloved daughter." Alternatively, the leader could say, "We are known and loved by God," followed by the group repeating, "We are God's beloved daughters."

Close with this litany[6] from *Sing the Story* #201:

Leader: All the broken hearts shall rejoice;
all those who are heavy laden,
whose eyes are tired and do not see,
shall be lifted up to meet with
the Motherly Healer.

People: **The battered souls and bodies shall be healed:**
the hungry shall be fed;
the imprisoned shall be set free.

All: *All earthly children shall regain joy*
in the reign of the just and loving One
coming for you
coming for me
in this time
in this world.

....
[1] *The New Oxford Annotated Bible with the Apocrypha, New Revised Standard Version* (Oxford: Oxford University Press, 1994).

[2] Mark 4:40.

[3] Ched Myers, *Binding the Strong Man*, (Maryknoll, NY: Orbis Books, 2003), 201.

[4] Mark 1:40-42.

[5] See Numbers 19:11-13 for instructions about uncleanness from touching dead bodies.

[6] Extracted from the poem "Prophesy" by Sun Ai Pak, published in *In God's Image*, April 1986, Asian Women's Resource Center for Culture and Theology. Used by permission.

Speaking Boldly: The Syrophoenician Woman

READING: Mark 7:24-30

OVERVIEW

We know little about this woman except that she was a Syrophoenician Gentile from the region of Tyre. Tyre was a city along the Mediterranean Sea, some 40 miles northwest of Nazareth. Jesus had gone there to rest with his disciples. King Herod had just killed John the Baptist, and religious leaders from Jerusalem had been pestering Jesus about why his disciples did not wash their hands properly.

Just a bit earlier Jesus had also tried to get away, but the crowds—over 5,000 people—followed him. Then he crossed the lake and still the people came. When they recognized Jesus, they rushed about everywhere and brought the sick to him. So when Jesus went to Tyre, he was seeking a safer, quieter place where he could escape notice, at least for a little while.

But now here was this *woman*, this *Gentile* woman, who dared to enter the home where he was staying. She came right into their midst and bowed down at his feet, much like Jairus had just done earlier. But Jesus did not respond to her as he did to Jairus, and initially appeared to turn her away.

VISUAL: a megaphone or microphone

GATHERING

Recall a time when you've felt especially driven to speak up, to step out of your comfort zone and do something that felt bold or uncomfortable. What was your biggest fear? What happened?

How do you think of obedience to God's Spirit? When does God honor meekness and when does God want boldness? What settings encourage you to say what is on your heart and when does this feel risky?

DEEPENING

In trying to understand this story, it is helpful to know more about that time and culture, and to realize just how much this woman had stepped out of line. Ched Myers explains that "no woman, and especially a Gentile, unknown and unrelated to this Jew, would have dared invade his privacy at home to seek a favor."[1] Mary Talbot also notes that in honorable families, it was the "responsibility of the father" or other male relative to care for the family.[2]

So this woman's actions took enormous courage. Rather than waiting patiently outside in the shadows, or getting in line outside the door, this woman made herself visible and spoke up, even though she hadn't been asked or given permission.

And then Jesus tried to turn her away! One wonders if she had prepared herself for this. It must have felt so humiliating.

Was she tempted to run away, hoping few people had noticed? Or did this make her even more determined to find help for her daughter?

In any case, this woman stood firm. She took Jesus' words and answered back: "Lord, even the dogs under the table eat the children's crumbs." This is quite unusual. As one commentator notes, Jesus is often seen arguing with those in power and winning the dispute with a "snappy saying." In this story alone, the snappy comeback is not made by Jesus but by this unnamed Gentile woman.[3]

In this story alone, the snappy comeback is not made by Jesus but by this unnamed Gentile woman.

This time, Jesus honored her. He honored her persistence and forthrightness. So often we fear God will punish us for being honest, for questioning, for sharing our deepest feelings and thoughts. But this is okay with God. Jesus actually granted this woman's request because of what she said: "*For saying that*, you may go—the demon has left your daughter."

But there is more. Soon after this, Jesus went on to teach and feed another large crowd. This time there were more than 4,000 people and it was in Gentile territory. So there were two feedings, one for Jews and one for Gentiles. Interestingly, the Greek word for being "filled" is the same word Jesus used when he told the woman, "Let the children be *fed* first."[4]

So this second feeding miracle clearly showed that God wants *all* to be fed or satisfied. The Gentiles did not have to settle for leftover crumbs; they could be filled too and there would still be seven baskets left over.

This is truly a comforting message. God wants to offer wholeness to everyone. And there is enough in God's economy to feed all God's children. But this message can also be threatening, especially to those who believe there is only enough for some: for those who do things the "right" way, who have the "right" skin color or nationality.

This bold woman showed, however, that we can all come to God and ask for help. We may need healing for ourselves. We may seek healing for others. No matter what, we can trust in God's deep, abundant love and know God will honor such love and honesty. God wants to provide for all.

INTEGRATING

1 . What is comforting to you in this story? What raises questions? If you could talk with Jesus honestly and boldly, what would you want to say or ask?

2 . As you consider your family or community, who is crying out for healing? Who is being excluded or fed the leftover crumbs? How might God start to bring wholeness in this situation?

3 . Sometimes there are barriers we do not intend because life experiences and assumptions can be so different. How do we invite those who've been outside our circles to share their observations and insights? Or if we have been marginalized, what do we need in order to speak up and share what is on our hearts? How can we be allies to one another and make sure all voices are heard and taken seriously?

CLOSING

Sing or read one of these songs:
    "Healer of Our Every Ill" (*Hymnal: A Worship Book* #377)
    "There Is More Love Somewhere" (*Sing the Journey* #109)

Close by praying this prayer[5] from *Hymnal: A Worship Book* #735:

> *Transforming God,*
>> *you come to us in expected and unexpected ways,*
>>> *desiring to be known yet remaining a mystery.*
> *Make your presence known among us.*
> *Confront us.*
> *Wrestle with us.*
> *Change us, through Jesus Christ, our Lord. Amen.*

....

[1] Ched Myers, *Binding the Strong Man* (Maryknoll, NY: Orbis Books, 2003), 203.

[2] Mary Ann Talbot, "Mark," in *The Women's Bible Commentary*, ed. Carol A. Newsom and Sharon H. Ringe (Louisville: Westminster/John Knox Press, 1992), 269.

[3] Joanna Dewey, "The Gospel of Mark," in *Searching the Scriptures, vol. 2: A Feminist Commentary*, ed. Elizabeth Schuessler Fiorenza (New York: Crossroad, 1994), 484.

[4] Ibid., 188.

[5] By Rebecca Slough, adaptation copyright © 1992 by The Hymnal Project. Used by permission.

Ten . . . .

Surprising Witness:
The Samaritan Woman

READING: John 4:1-42

OVERVIEW

Jesus' visit with the Samaritan woman at the well not only astonished the disciples; Jesus also surprised her. She too had trouble believing that Jesus would talk with her or accept anything she had to offer. Yet, she and Jesus went on to have a remarkable conversation, one of the longest Jesus had with anyone in the Gospels.

Is this why she is not named? To remind all of us that no matter what others say, Jesus values everyone? He invites each of us to believe and follow him, and to share our gifts with others. Even when we feel like outsiders, Jesus reaches out and brings us into the circle of disciples.

VISUAL: a clay jar or a bucket filled with water and enough mugs or cups for everyone present

GATHERING

Recall a time when you felt especially thirsty. What were your thoughts and feelings? What quenched your thirst and how did that feel? Have there been times when you have also felt spiritually parched? What brought relief and satisfied your thirst in those situations?

Try to place yourself in the shoes of this woman. What thoughts and feelings might you have had as you saw this Jewish stranger sitting at the well where you needed to draw water? How would you have responded to his questions and statements?

DEEPENING

Much has been written about this woman, especially that she had five husbands and was now living with a sixth man. Yet, in that time women had little control and few options when it came to marriage and sexual relationships.

Likely, her situation was similar to that of Tamar, who, after her husband's death, was required to marry one of his brothers.

Likely, her situation was similar to that of Tamar, who, after her husband's death, was required to marry one of his brothers in order to have a child who could claim her husband's name and inheritance.[1] Unfortunately, Onan balked at this because he did not want to support such a child. When he then died, Tamar's father-in-law, Judah, feared she had caused these deaths and was reluctant to give her another husband.

Did the Samaritan woman have a similar experience? While six brothers seems excessive, disease and violence were common in that time and this poor woman may have been passed from one brother to another. But did the final one refuse to marry her because he too feared death?

One can only imagine how difficult life was for this woman. If she had indeed lost five husbands, she must have felt terrible grief. Perhaps people gossiped about why all of these men had died. No doubt she too wondered why her family had experienced so much misfortune. Was she to blame? Had she committed some terrible sin for which she was being punished? Was this why she came to the well alone, at midday, rather than with the other women in the town?

Given all this, it is interesting to note the contrast between her encounter with Jesus and that of Nicodemus in John 3. Briefly:

- Nicodemus has a name; she does not.

- He is male; she is female.

- He is a respected Jewish leader; she is a despised Samaritan.

- He comes to Jesus secretly by night; she talks with Jesus in public, in full daylight.

- He appears puzzled and full of questions; Jesus reveals himself to her as the Messiah, and she goes into her village to urge others to meet Jesus.

Despite these differences, their discussions with Jesus both centered on what it means to truly worship God, in spirit and truth. Fortunately, this woman was able to perceive that God might be doing something new, something even more powerful than settling the age-old dispute between Jews and Samaritans about where they should worship. As Jesus had told Nicodemus, God's wind, God's spirit "blows where it chooses." We cannot control it or decide who will receive it.

Surely, this was good news for one who felt cast out and who had little influence in her community. No doubt she thirsted for love and acceptance, for assurance that God had not abandoned her but would always be with her, as a "spring of living water" to give her life and love that would never end.

Initially so amazed by Jesus, this woman then surprised everyone by rushing into the town to share what she had experienced. Like John the Baptist, Andrew, and Philip in John 1, she became a witness, telling others about Jesus, so that the number of his followers grew.

INTEGRATING

1. Have you ever had a surprising encounter with God? How was that similar to or different than this woman's experience?

2. Who in your community, like the Samaritan woman, would be especially surprised by Jesus' willingness to talk with them and welcome their contributions? How would they find life-giving water?

3. Despite the differences between Nicodemus and the Samaritan woman, the gospel of John reports that both became Jesus' disciples and supported his work.[2] How are you like Nicodemus? The Samaritan woman? What unique gift do you bring to Jesus?

4. When have you felt God quenching your thirst, physically, emotionally, spiritually? In what situations do you still long for the water of life? If helpful, create a poem, song, or drawing to express these longings and bring them to God in prayer.

CLOSING

Pray the prayer[3] in *Sing the Story* #162:

> Leader: God of all who thirst,
>
> our hearts are parched from wandering in deserts
>
> far from your life-giving springs.
>
> Call us to your well.

> **All: Fill our cups with your grace.**
>
> **Let your love overflow in our hearts,**
>
> **and make us fully alive. Amen.**

Pass cups of water around the circle and drink together. Then sing or read one of these songs:
   "Rain Down" (*Sing the Journey* #49)
   "O Let All Who Thirst" (*Hymnal: A Worship Book* #495)

---

[1] Genesis 38:6-11; Deuteronomy 25:5-10; Ruth 4:1-12. While this practice seems foreign to us, it was apparently still common in Jesus' time, as seen in a question from the Sadducees. Trying to refute Jesus' teaching on resurrection, they asked who would be the real husband to a woman who had married seven brothers, each of whom had died in turn. (See Mark 12:18-23; Luke 20:27-35.)

[2] John 7:50-52; 19:39-42.

[3] Ruth Yoder, from *Words for Worship* edited by Arlene M. Mark. Copyright © 1996 by Herald Press, Scottdale, PA. Used by permission.

Brave Friends:
Mary and Martha

READING: John 11:1-44; 12:1-11; Luke 10:38-42

OVERVIEW

It is truly remarkable how the Gospels describe Jesus' friendship with Mary and Martha. From what we know of that
culture, men and women rarely interacted with one another
except in the context of family or marriage. Yet both of these
women welcomed Jesus and spoke freely with him. They
asked questions and raised concerns, as if they were not at all
intimidated by him or the other disciples, or felt the need to
keep themselves apart.

Jesus also welcomed both Martha and Mary as disciples and
treated them with the utmost respect. Contrary to all expectations, he praised Mary for sitting with the men and learning
as a full disciple and urged Martha to do the same.[1] Then, in
John's gospel, Martha is the one who talked with him about
life, death, and resurrection. She (and not Peter) is the one
who publicly declared him to be the "Messiah, the Son of
God, the one coming into the world."[2]

VISUAL: a collection of friendship bracelets, enough for
each person

GATHERING

As you read these passages, pay special attention to the conversations Jesus had with these sisters. What stands out to you as you read these accounts? If you could talk with Mary and Martha, what would you ask them?

What have you heard about Mary and Martha? With whom do you identify most, and why?

DEEPENING

According to these gospel accounts, Jesus seemed to have a special friendship with this family. Although he traveled all over Judea, Galilee, and Samaria, spending time in many homes, we rarely know the names of the host or hostess. So this family must have held a unique place in Jesus' life.

Perhaps their home felt like a safe haven, a place where Jesus and the disciples could relax and rest in relative peace and security. This would have been especially important as tensions increased between Jesus and the religious authorities in Jerusalem. Already in John 5, these leaders were seeking to kill Jesus, and later they actually picked up stones against him on two occasions.[3] In fact, just before Lazarus became sick, they tried again to arrest him. Jesus then withdrew across the Jordan River to a more secluded place, roughly 20 miles from Jerusalem.[4]

So this friendship was forged in a difficult context. Danger followed Jesus and his disciples, and fear filled the air. What would happen to Jesus and his friends if the authorities found them? When Lazarus became ill and grew steadily worse, Martha and Mary feared for his life too. No doubt, they also feared for themselves; if Lazarus died, they would be left vulnerable and without the security and support a man provided in that society.

Perhaps this is why there is so much emotion in this story. Martha and Mary were upset about the threats Jesus was facing, threats that forced him into hiding and out of reach when they needed him. When Lazarus died, they may have also wondered if God had deserted them. Jesus had given them such hope, such assurance that things could change. But now he was far away and their brother was gone too.

When Lazarus died, they may have also wondered if God had deserted them.

Of course, the text shows Jesus wanting to demonstrate God's glory and power over death. Still, it must have been hard for them. When Jesus finally came, both sisters lamented, "Lord, if you had been here, my brother would not have died." Jesus too was greatly disturbed and wept with the others because of all that had happened.

In the end, God's power was stronger than death, able to bring Lazarus back to life, and many came to believe in Jesus. Yet the threats continued to escalate until Jesus went into hiding again.[5] Now Lazarus was at risk too, since his restoration caused many to believe.[6]

Even so, this family continued to host Jesus in their home. Interestingly, this time Martha served without complaint. And Mary again did an unusual thing, anointing Jesus' feet with perfume. Scholars debate what this anointing meant, but it certainly pointed to her love for Jesus and recognition that he was about to die. Similar to Martha's earlier declaration, it was also a sign of her faith in him as the true Messiah, the "Anointed" One.[7]

Although our gospel accounts do not mention this family again, one can imagine they were well-known in the early church. Since Mary and Martha figure so strongly in these stories, they were also likely leaders, fondly remembered for the way they hosted Jesus and the disciples.

INTEGRATING

1. What are the key ingredients of friendship? Which of these elements show up in Jesus' friendship with Martha and Mary?

2. To what extent does friendship require courage? When have you been brave for your friends? When have they been brave for you?

3. Mary and Martha both appeared free to speak with Jesus and ask questions. What are other examples from Scripture of people asking God questions or sharing deep emotions and even doubt? When is it good to ask questions and when is it better to rest in faith and trust?

4. Martha and Mary learned to know Jesus in a context where gender roles were very clear. How did these expectations affect their relationships? To what extent did each of them accept or challenge these roles?

CLOSING

Sing or read one of these songs:
> "What a Friend We Have in Jesus" (*Hymnal: A Worship Book* #573)
> "Woza Nomthwalo Wakho" / "Come, Bring Your Burdens to God" (*Sing the Story* #50)

Share a friendship bracelet with each woman, asking each to help the next woman tie it on her wrist. Close by saying this blessing together and to one another:

Thank you for welcoming,
Thank you for serving,
Thank you for asking questions,
Thank you for listening,
Thank you for blessing me,
Thank you for being a friend.

....
[1] Luke 10:38-42. Bailey explains that "to 'sit at the feet' of a rabbi meant to become a disciple of a rabbi." Kenneth E. Bailey, "Women in the New Testament: A Middle Eastern Cultural View," *Theology Matters*, Jan./Feb. 2000, 2, http://www.theologymatters.com/JanFeb001.PDF.

[2] John 11:27.

[3] John 5:16-18; 8:59; 10:31. See also Luke 6:11.

[4] John 7:25-32; 10:39-40.

[5] John 11:54-57.

[6] John 12:10-11.

[7] John 1:41. See also Acts 4:27 and 10:38, for a description of how Jesus was "anointed" by God.

Twelve. . . . .

Strong Partner: Priscilla

READING: Acts 18:1-6, 18-19, 24-28;
Romans 16:3-5

OVERVIEW

Many of us have heard about Paul's missionary journeys and his coworkers Barnabus, Silas, Luke, and Timothy. We have also heard much about Paul's writings that restricted women's roles and ministries.

Less attention has been focused on how Paul worked with women and expressed much warmth and appreciation for their ministry. One of the most prominent was Priscilla, who, along with her husband, Aquila, traveled with Paul on his second missionary journey and then stayed behind in Ephesus to encourage the believers there. Paul mentioned this couple several times in his letters, so they seem to have played an especially significant role in his life.[1]

Paul worked with other women too. In Romans 16, he sent greetings to 10 women out of a total of 27 people. In addition to Priscilla, these included Phoebe,[2] Mary,[3] Junia,[4] Tryphaena and Tryphosa, Persis, Julia, Rufus's mother, and Nereus's sister. In 1 Corinthians 1:11, Paul noted that he had received reports from those in Chloe's household. And in Philippians he named Euodia and Syntyche as two women who "struggled beside" him in the work of the gospel.[5]

Because we are so far removed from that culture and language, and no longer recognize which are male and female names, it is easy to overlook these women, who were active throughout the early church alongside Paul and other church leaders. It is essential for us to recover this history in order to better understand the full gospel message and how it applies to us today.

VISUAL: a circle made of paper cutouts of people holding hands or a collection of tea-light candles, enough for each woman to light one

GATHERING

Make a list of women from the early church.[6] What do you know about them and what they did? If you could talk with one of them, whom would you choose and what would you ask her?

Read the passages about Priscilla and Aquila in one sitting. What stands out or surprises you? Try to imagine Paul living, working, and traveling with this couple. What kinds of conversations did they have? How did they divide the work? What kind of worship and learning did they share together?

DEEPENING

As recorded in Acts 18:2, Paul met Aquila and Priscilla in Corinth, where they had settled after the Jews were expelled from Rome. Paul ended up living and working with them, and when he set out for Syria, they went along. After stopping in Ephesus, Priscilla and Aquila stayed behind to strengthen and encourage the believers there. They hosted the church in their home and appeared to be active leaders in the congregation. When the enthusiastic and eloquent teacher Apollos came to Ephesus, they were the ones who gave him a more accurate understanding of the gospel.

It is intriguing to imagine what those conversations were like. We do not know what kind of schooling Priscilla and Aquila had, but Apollos likely had access to good educational opportunities. Not only was he "well-versed in the Scriptures" but he was also from Alexandria, "the intellectual center of the empire," where the Greek translation of the Old Testament had been produced.[7] So it likely took some courage for this couple to take this charismatic man aside and let him know

It likely took some courage for this couple to take this charismatic man aside and let him know he was missing some knowledge.

he was missing some knowledge. Even more surprising is that Priscilla's name is mentioned first. This is unusual even today and may indicate she was the more visible leader and the one who took the initiative in giving this instruction.

This teaching effort with Apollos was effective. He was able to gain the support of the Ephesian believers, and when he wanted to travel to Corinth in Achaia, they sent along letters of introduction. There, he "greatly helped" those believers and played a significant role in those churches, on a par with Paul's ministry.[8]

Paul also mentioned that Priscilla and Aquila took risks for him and the gospel. While he does not give details, Acts 18:12-16 recounts how Jews in Corinth brought him before Roman authorities, accusing him of breaking the law. Then in Ephesus, the silversmiths almost started a riot because they feared Paul's ministry would destroy their business.[9] Were

Priscilla and Aquila also threatened during these incidents due to their close connection to Paul? Or perhaps there was another occasion in which they endangered their lives to help Paul.

Another interesting aspect of this couple is that they are always mentioned together, one of few husband and wife teams mentioned in the New Testament. It would be wonderful to know more about them and how they worked together. Did they always teach together? Did they have children? How did they decide who would do what? While we can never know these details, we can be grateful for their ministry and the encouragement and challenge they give us today.

INTEGRATING

1. What sermons or lessons have you heard about Priscilla or other female leaders in the early church? If you had the opportunity, what sermon or lesson would you like to give?

2. What additional study would you like to do about women in the Bible? Are there also women in your community you would like to interview and learn from?

3. What are the unique gifts men and women bring to the church? How can men and women be partners today in sharing the gospel?

CLOSING

Sing or read one of these songs:
"Here, O Lord, Your Servants Gather" (Hymnal: A Worship Book #7)
"God the Spirit, Guide and Guardian" (Hymnal: A Worship Book #632)

Pray the prayer in *Sing the Journey* #167, or pray this one:

Faithful God, thank you for all who have served you over the centuries: women like Priscilla, men like Aquila. Thank you for their example. Help us to also find our place in your family as beloved daughters and sons. Through Jesus Christ our Lord, Amen.

....

[1] Romans 16:3-5; 1 Corinthians 16:19; 2 Timothy 4:19.

[2] Phoebe likely carried the letter to Rome, as Paul commends her to them and urges them to welcome and assist her. Many translations refer to her as a deacon, but the Greek word *diakonos* is translated as "minister" elsewhere (e.g., 2 Corinthians 3:6; 11:15; Ephesians 6:21; Colossians 1:7; 4:7).

[3] Mary and others are described as "working hard." Paul used the Greek word for "worked hard" to describe "work for the gospel" (e.g., 1 Corinthians 15:10; 16:15-16; Galatians 4:11; Philippians 2:16; Colossians 1:29; 1 Timothy 4:10; 5:17). See David M. Scholer, "Paul's Women Co-Workers in the Ministry of the Church," *The Wisdom of Daughters*, ed. Reta Halteman Finger and Kari Sandhaas (Philadelphia: Innisfree Press, 2001), 76.

[4] Although some translations use the male name Junias, Bailey explains that all of the early manuscripts and church fathers read this name as feminine. Not until late in the 13th century did some manuscripts and translations switch to Junias. This was done without any evidence and despite the fact that such a name was unknown in any Latin or Greek text, whereas the female version of the name, Junia, was quite common in classical literature. See Kenneth E. Bailey, "Women in the New Testament: A Middle Eastern Cultural View," *Theology Matters*, Jan./Feb. 2000, 4, http://www.theologymatters.com/JanFeb001.PDF.

[5] Philippians 4:2-3.

[6] See especially Acts 9:36; 12:12; 16:11-15; 17:4, 12, 34; and 21:8-9.

[7] Chalmer E Faw, *Acts*, Believers Church Bible Commentary (Scottdale, PA: Herald Press, 1993), 212.

[8] 1 Corinthians 3:5-9.

[9] Acts 19:23-41.

Thirteen ....

Honoring Courageous Women (Closing Worship)

VISUAL FOCUS

Bring 20 sets of footprints with the names of all the women studied in this series written on them. Give these to the 12 women who will read a part in the litany so that after each woman reads her phrase, she can place her footprints on a path leading to or from your circle.

You may also want to display the visuals from previous sessions around the room as a reminder of your journey with these courageous women of the Bible.

Finally, bring drawings of additional footprints and invite each woman to cut out several more. Each woman should have at least three sets of footprints to use toward the end of the session.

SONG: "Come, Come Ye Saints" (*Hymnal: A Worship Book* #425)

GATHERING

Leader: We have walked with many women over these weeks,
women from long ago, women today.
We carry all of them in our hearts.

Leader: We remember Hagar.

Woman 1: Hagar, who feared that all was lost but was seen and found by God.

Leader: We remember Shiphrah and Puah.

Woman 2: Shiphrah and Puah, who revered God and dared to disobey the mighty Pharaoh.

Leader: We remember Mahlah, Noah, Hoglah, Milcah, and Tirzah.

Woman 3: Mahlah, Noah, Hoglah, Milcah, and Tirzah, who saw that something was wrong and sought justice together.

Leader: We remember Naomi, Orpah, and Ruth.

Woman 4: Naomi, Orpah, and Ruth, who experienced tragedy and hardship but never gave up hope, and who loved and supported one another as they were able.

Leader: We remember Huldah.

Woman 5: Huldah, who served God as a prophet and spoke truth to the king.

Leader: We remember Vashti.

Woman 6: Vashti, who claimed her worth as a person, who honored herself and refused to be an object.

Leader: We remember Mary, Jesus' mother.

Woman 7: Mary, whose faith was undaunted by struggle and who kept believing God loved her and would bring peace and wholeness to her people.

Leader: We remember the woman with the flow of blood.

Woman 8: The woman who dared to seek healing, even if it meant breaking the rules.

Leader: We remember the Syrophoenician woman.

Woman 9: The foreign woman who spoke up boldly for her daughter and would not back away.

Leader: We remember the Samaritan woman.

Woman 10: The surprised woman who asked questions and then witnessed to others in her town.

Leader: We remember Mary and Martha.

Woman 11: Martha and Mary, two of Jesus' loyal disciples and brave friends.

Leader: We remember Priscilla.

Woman 12: Priscilla, the strong teacher who worked together with Aquila and Paul in sharing the gospel.

Leader: We have walked with many women over these weeks,
women from long ago, women today.
We carry all of them in our hearts.

CONFESSING

Leader: Dear God, thank you for these women who have inspired us.
We lament that we have heard so little about them.
We grieve that we do not know all of their names.

All: *Help us to honor them now.*

Leader: Dear God, we know many people are still forgotten, many women are still overlooked, and we do not know their names.

All: *Forgive us, God. Help us to see them. Help us to ask for their names. Help us to remember and honor them too.*

Leader: Dear God, we confess that we also feel forgotten at times. We sometimes feel overlooked and invisible and wonder where you are.

All: *Help us, dear God. Help us trust in your love. Help us know that you walk with us wherever we go. Help us to honor ourselves.*

RESPONDING

Invite everyone to reflect on which of these women was especially memorable or inspiring to them. Also, what lesson or commitment will they take with them in the next weeks or months? Are there other women in the Bible they would like to learn about? If this is comfortable for your group, have them share answers to these questions in pairs. Another option is to invite everyone to write their answers on a slip of paper to take with them.

Also, ask everyone to think of women who have been important in their lives. Who has inspired them and encouraged them? Invite each woman to take the footprints they cut out and write the names on the cutouts. Finally, ask them to write their own name on a set of footprints. Place these footprints on the path, as you sing together "Hamba Nathi" / "Come, Walk with Us" (*Sing the Journey* # 2).

CLOSING

Sing or read one of these songs:

"God of Grace, God of Glory" (*Hymnal: A Worship Book* #366)

"God of the Bible" (*Sing the Journey* #27)

"My Soul Cries Out" (*Sing the Story* #124)

"Woman in the Night" (*Hymnal: A Worship Book* #223)

Read a litany[1] in *Sing the Story* #199:

Leader: For all the saints who went before us
who have spoken to our hearts and touched us
with your fire,

All: *we praise you, O God.*

Leader: For all the saints who live beside us
whose weaknesses and strengths are woven
with our own,

All: *we praise you, O God.*

Leader: For all the saints who live beyond us
who challenge us to change the world with
them,

All: *we praise you, O God. Amen.*

Or pray together:

Dear loving God, thank you that we can join this stream of women, this cloud of witnesses and saints who have gone before us on this journey of faith. We also thank you for those who walk beside us, who encourage and challenge us each day. Help us to walk joyfully, confidently, and faithfully so that those who come after us may also find your love and follow on the way. Give us courage; give us hope; give us joy. Amen.

....
[1] Janet Morley, © 2013 Christian Aid, used by permission.

About Mennonite Women Canada

As each has received a gift, employ it for one another, as good stewards of God's varied grace. —1 Peter 4:10

Mission statement

Mennonite Women Canada encourages women to:

- nurture their life in Christ

- acknowledge and share their gifts

- hear and support each other

- serve and minister across the street and around the world

We commit ourselves to:

- Promote spiritual growth through Bible study, prayer and fellowship.

- Discern and nurture women's gifts and skills for leadership and service in the local church, the community, and the world.

- Build relationships and networks for support, affirmation, discernment, witness, service, and celebration.

- Support and strengthen the missional outreach of Mennonite Church Canada.

We do this through:

- Publication of an annual Bible Study Guide as partners with MW USA.

- Providing scholarships for women studying Anabaptist theology at a master's level though our Spiritual Growth Assistance Fund.

- Connecting women across Canada via our semiannual newsletter, *Connections*, and bimonthly pages in the Canadian Mennonite magazine under the headline "Women Walking Together in Faith."

- Supporting and encouraging women working in Mennonite Church Canada's ministries through our Pennies and Prayer Legacy Fund.

- Maintaining a web page at http://www.mennonitechurch.ca/mwc/ and a blog at http://mennowomencanada.blogspot.com/.

- Connecting with and supporting the provincial/area women's organizations through our executive meetings in March and at Mennonite Church Canada Assembly sessions.

We as Mennonite Women Canada are striving to do God's will and work where we are to the best of our ability. You too can be a part!

More information is available at our website (see address above).

Connect with us on our blog (see address above).

Contact the President at presmwcanada@gmail.com or write to Mennonite Women Canada c/o Mennonite Church Canada 600 Shaftesbury Blvd. Winnipeg, MB R3P 0M4.

About Mennonite Women USA

Jesus said: "I am the vine. You are the branches." —John 15:5

Mission statement

Our mission at Mennonite Women USA is to empower women and women's groups as we nurture our life in Christ through studying the Bible, using our gifts, hearing each other, and engaging in mission and service.

In living our mission, Mennonite Women USA:

- Connects globally by funding scholarships for women worldwide for church leadership training through our **International Women's Fund**.

- Equips women for caring ministry through **Sister Care seminars**. Sister Care validates women's gifts of caring and equips them to respond more effectively and confidently to the needs of others in their lives and in the congregation.

- Resources women's groups across the United States through leadership training, an annual Anabaptist Bible study guide, and *Timbrel* magazine. Sister Care seminars are hosted by area conference women.

- Speaks prophetically and shares stories of women of all ages and backgrounds through **Timbrel magazine**, the publication of Mennonite Women USA. *Timbrel* is published quarterly and invites women to be "in conversation together with God."

- Fosters relationships around the world through the **Sister-Link program**—emphasizing mutual giving and receiving and validating a wide variety of gifts. Sister-Links connect women through prayer, letter writing, sharing resources, and face-to-face visits.

- Cosponsors **Women in Conversation retreats** every two years in the East and the Midwest—a time for spiritual nourishment, reflection with God, and warm fellowship with other women.

Vision statement

Mennonite Women USA invites women across generations, cultures, and places to share and honor our stories, care for each other, and express our prophetic voice boldly as we seek to follow Christ.

We'd love to tell you more about our ministry.

Learn more about Mennonite Women USA programs—and get a little lift in your day—by signing up for our free monthly e-letter, "A Postcard & a Prayer." Just send your name, address, and email to office@MennoniteWomenUSA.org.

You may also access our website for our latest news and stories: www.MennoniteWomenUSA.org.

Mennonite Women USA
718 N. Main St.
Newton, KS 67114-1819
316.281.4396 or 866.866.2872, ext. 34396
office@MennoniteWomenUSA.org

About the writer

*L*inda Gehman Peachey is a writer and editor from Lancaster, Pennsylvania. Most recently, she wrote the booklet *Created Equal, Women and Men in the Image of God* (Mennonite Central Committee) and edited *With the Word: Acts* and *With the Word: Isaiah* (MennoMedia). Linda graduated from Anabaptist Mennonite Biblical Seminary with a master of divinity degree in 2004.

From 2004 to 2011, Linda was director of women's advocacy at Mennonite Central Committee U.S., working to address sexism and violence against women and children. Previously, she and her husband, Titus, were codirectors of MCC U.S. Peace and Justice Ministries and corepresentatives for MCC's development aid program in Laos.

Linda and Titus live in Lancaster City and are active members at East Chestnut Street Mennonite Church. They have two adult daughters and enjoy visiting them in Chicago and Guatemala. Linda also loves to read, hike, and spend time with friends.

Linda continues to ponder what it means to follow Jesus in these days of so much terror and hope. She has found it especially inspiring to explore women's stories in the Bible and learn more about how they met the challenges of their time. Even when their names are not recorded, it is encouraging to know their experiences were not lost. They remind us that everyone is important to the story. All are invited to be disciples and join in the movement toward God's surprising, upside-down vision of peace and wholeness on the earth.